Making the Life with the Life Giver

It is now Audition

By

Bernard Benson Sarfo

Also by Bernard Benson Sarfo

The Fact Among Facts (1st)
The Fact Among Facts

Standalone
The Youth Murderer
Be Original Not a Copy
The Christians Science or Scholarship
Precious than Paradise
Habit Makes Future
A shelter from storm and rain
The Science of Life
The Strongest Lion Knockback
The Perfect and Inspiring City
Above Hope, Faith and Love
The Hero's Brave Decisions
The Weakest Among Plants
The Hero's Brave Decisions
Doing Above The Ability
The Wisdom Beyond Power And Greatness

Heavier Than the Heavens
The Academics Brains and Recreation Logics
The Strange Voice
The Chaotic World
Don't Miss Your Flight
Let the Nations Ponder
You Are Your Thoughts
I AM has sent me to you
Life Tools
The Fact Among Facts
You Are Glorified
The Life Cinema
The Victims of Lifelong Slavery
The Beauty behind Her Ladyship
The Gorgeous and Vigorous City
What Is His Name?
Making the Life with the Life Giver

Dedication

I dedicate this book to everyone in the world today and wish them courage!

'When wisdom entered into your heart, and knowledge is pleasant unto your soul, discretion shall preserve you, understanding shall keep you' (Proverbs 2:10, 11).

Introduction

Oh how can a baby live alone without his or her mother guidance? Who have been able to live without mother or father before? Who has not been child before?

Can a man produce children without a woman? Can one man build a whole city without other hands? It is impossible to live without God or survive without air?

Do not challenge or annoy that you can do by your own strength. I have seen that, no one can survive without air, so it is that; without God no one can live. Many think that, it is by their power that they exist.

Your life is not yours that you can do for your own best. It is not in your hands to control air to move in the direction you want it. You are nothing and you cannot be anything without God.

It is not by power or strength to do; but by His Spirit. If I challenge, I will fail without His aid. Without Christ you can do nothing. I cannot; dare, to do without God. If you challenge, you will fail. Our only hope and life is Christ. Without Him no one will be accepted by God. It is not by our strength but by His grace that we live and have our being.

As the world came by the power and the word of God; so we can survive and have our being through His word. Without Him we cannot survive. Do not challenge that it is by your own strength.

It is not but by His grace. You shall be fruitless without His aid and you will be as nothing without His grace. You are not alone; your creator is still holding you and cares for you. He will not forget you or forsake you.

He knows the thought He has for you. It is a thought of peace but not of evil to give hope and future with abundance. You cannot; dare, walk alone. You shall fail by your own strength but you will win by His strength and power.

He has prepared everything necessary for your life and wishes you well. What you need is to trust Him and depend on Him. He will not leave you nor forsake you. It is not your duty to care for yourself, but it is your duty only to trust and obey Him. You shall not flop.

The world has totally changed from it state. The time is far more spent and days are now over. There is nothing good again, all things have changed and there is no better time again.

There is cry everywhere on the globe. Many people are dying without hope. There is no time again. What is going on now? What I mine seeing? Who is coming and what is going to happen?

Oh who knows what will happen after this time? There is no comfort and no peace at all. What can I say and what I mine going to say? The world is dark and there is no good at all.

Who will comfort us and what will be the results at the end of condition that we are all going through? What have you notice and what have you considered?

What will be the end of each other and what will be the reward after this? What is the time now, oh keeper? Will you be able to pass through all these conditions that are going on?

Will you be accepted by the Master when He comes? What will be your condition and your reward? Will you be please the

Master? Where will you stand? This is the time of salvation; this is the time of grace.

What are you doing? How will you response when you call the by the Master? Keep watch and stay safe and then practice what is good. There is no time again. What have you imagine?

Contents

1. I cannot walk alone

Oh how can I live without you and go without your presence? I cannot; dare, walk alone. I need you every day oh precious savior. It is your voice that gives me peace.

My hope is within you and my happiness is to see your face. Please, do not leave me alone and do not turn your eyes from me. My hope is within you. Oh Lord! I cannot go without you or seeing you beside me.

The world is dark and fear allover; I cannot see ahead, shadows across the sky, thunder and lightning are sounding like the waves of sea. Oh Lord! I cannot go without you, walk with me.

Hold my weak hand and lead me on my way. Show me the way I should go and lead me to the end. I cannot; dare, walk alone, Lord Walk with me.

My life is not certain; I cannot see ahead, it seems I am very late them everyone on earth. Oh Lord! It is not late for you, do something and give me strength to hope for. Walk with me. Many things are fighting against me; I cannot move without you Lord, walk with me. In fact, you cannot do without God; neither can you go without Him. Though, your life seems negative; as if all things were against you.

You do not know what to do and do not know where to go. It is hard for you to survive and worse for you to tell your story. There are many things that fighting against you.

Your troubles are filled up and worse things always happen to you. It is not your fight; you cannot do anything about it. Leave to God and be at peace.

For you cannot; dare, fight alone. Let Him fight for you. It shall be well. It is not your duty to fight for your own, but it is your duty to trust and obey His word. That is, your only security is to trust and obey Him.

There is no other way to be happy in Jesus, but only to trust and obey Him. Your life is not yours to plan for it greatness and beauty. But leave everything to God and live as He has instructed you.

All things shall work together for your good according to His purpose for you. You cannot; dare, do for yourself by your own effort. You shall fail and be as nothing. Your life is in His hand and He can turn it as He wants. You have no control about your life but you can do something according to His will and pleasure to please Him.

Only avoid laziness and do what you can through His grace. He will take care of all and make things easier for you. You cannot; dare, do something without Christ.

He knows the plans He had for you; it is for your greatness and future expectation. Do not force yourself to be rich, nor rush for fame. It is not your duty, but your duty is to follow His step as He leads you. It shall be well.

Do your best and what you can and leave the rest to Him and then says, I have done as you instructed me. Lord it is your turn. Do not leave me alone and I cannot; walk alone.

Do not consider your beauty and greatness in future. But consider God first and all things shall be added for you. You cannot; dare, walk alone. He will be with you until the end of time.

2. The life is tough for me

Though, you have done your best as you can but things are not going well as you wish. You need to be tested by circumstances to see if you are fit to handle things well.

It is tough; it is a lesson for your maturity. You do not see clearly; it is not as you know already. Why things have change suddenly? Is it my sins or my destiny? Why these things? It is hard for me now.

What shall I do and come out from all these trials? Why things still the same? There is nothing that has change in my life. Still things are tough for me and I do not know why?

You need to be press and know what you can be used for. In life, lessons are our progress act which makes us who we are and what we can do more than imagine.

Our ways are not God ways or our thought His thoughts. He knows us more than we do. He created us and knows what is within us. Sin has changed our beauty and what we can do. We are like gold; we need to refine by fire, then to be useful for the Master. Whatever your lesson; makes you great and suits you for good use. Do not be worry when things went wrong. But be alert and know what the master have for you.

Do not guess or think of the outcome but be honest and stay cool until the end. It is for your good but not your wreck. You need to be fit for the position you about to be hold.

It is not what you think but it is His will to make you great and fit for good works. You cannot; dare, do it by your strength. He (God) will do it for you.

It is not your duty to stress yourself about world matters. But it is your duty to seek His kingdom first and then all things will be added for your good. Why is it hard for you? It means you are worthy to do and handle more.

You need to be trained for it and then set you for good works and victory. You cannot; it is tough for you, you wish to give up. You cannot entertain it again. You are tire of your situation.

Do not be afraid; it is for your good but not your ruin. Be faithful to the end; do not allow it for sin. Your trials are your master which teaches you how to hold yourself for great things. It is not for wreck but your fame. Let it not be a strange thing happens to you. But keep in mind that all things work good for God's people that are called be His purpose.

Leave everything to Him and be at peace; why are you challenging? You have something special to do for God and His people around you. It is you only that you can do that thing.

So, you must be trained for and make things well to suit the Master wishes. He will not leave you alone do by your strength. He has prepared the way you should do it with ease.

You will not get as you wish, but you will get it as God wishes. Without Him you can do nothing. You must be train for; else you will do foolish things which will lead you into destruction.

It is for your good that it has come so. In fact, my dear your life is not in your hands to make it as you wish. It is in the hands of God. Whatever transpires has a purpose for your life. It is for good and great expectation but not for your ruin. Keep it in mind and be honest to the end.

3. Without you I can do nothing

How can I do without you oh Lord? How can I go without you? I will lose; if I dare, Lord holds me firmly in this trouble world. What can I do Lord apart from you?

I cannot live without you and I cannot go without you. My ways are evil all day long. I am weak; I need your hands to support me. What can I do, that will appreciate you? My good works are like rag before you.

My ways are wrong and my doings are pretense. What can benefit me without you? Only you can do through me for your own appreciation. Our doings are always evil and our ways are trick.

We cannot do to appreciate God, unless He does through us. Never think you are without God or Christ. Our Life and ways are for Him and the world and everything in them are for Him.

He owns everything and through Him all things were made. In Him that we move and have our beings; He is our maker and savior. It is His will that we were created. In fact, we cannot live without God as human beings. Everyone must note that, without Christ; he or she is nothing. Apart from Him, we are nothing and cannot be counted as anything. Who are you and what can you do? He is the true vine and we are His branches.

Whatever the branch can do must come from the vine itself. The breaches have no root but it depend on the vine to survive. When one of the branches avoids the vine feed, it will collapse and then die.

This is how we live and move through our maker. If we avoid Him, we avoid life and wish to cease forever. You cannot do or live without Him. He is our source of life and everything we need.

Maybe you may try with your own effort, but what will be the end. It is even impossible for you to do without God. You should worry yourself anything, but leave to God and be at peace.

It shall be well and without Him, you can do nothing. Many people want to do great things by their own strength. But what will be the results? Do not think that you can do by your own might. It is not so, you cannot, except He (God) allows it. Else, it will avian in nothing. So, we are nothing without God and cannot be anything apart from Him. You should not boast on things that you have been able to do.

It is not by your strength; your wise or your ability. But it is by His grace that made that chance for you to do. You do not have any idea and do not own anything concerning your skills. You cannot without Him do something.

It is by the grace that He provides and then makes us do and move. It is His depth of mercy that we as sinners move and live. We have nothing to do about it.

He is our life and creator. He wants us good and wishes our best. It is not by your ability or strength, but it is His mercy and grace. I cannot do without you, Lord! Hold my hands and lead me. Without you; I will be nothing and cannot do for myself. It is only you can do through me. I cannot; dare, do without you! Please, do not leave me, be my guide and helper. I cannot; dare, do without you.

4. My life is yours

Oh Lord! Do not leave me, I am your son and my life is yours. It is now finished; my hope is gone. What will happen to me? Please, do not leave me; my life is yours.

It is now destroy; how can I get it back? My eyes is upon you; it is only you can do. My life is yours. Many people are seeking my fall and disgrace. My hope is gone; it is only you can do.

Please, do not leave me, my life is yours. I have wasted my time for nothing and people are laughing at me. What should I do? I am getting old and nothing shows my progress.

Only you can do. Please, do not abandon me, my life is yours. It is so that your life is not certain and it is seems it has ended. There is nothing show that you will be somebody at the end.

You have spent your time for nothing. But it is not late yet. There is hope for the hopeless. Let your pray be my life is yours; Lord do not leave but have mercy on me.

Your life must be certain in God but no other. The world has nothing for you. He can do beyond what you think or ask, it is not yet your time. But keep waiting and waiting. Do not destroy your beauty by bribe or any enticement. Only be faithful and do what you can.

Make your life His life; means surrender everything to Him and wait for His time. He will not fail you or forsake you. You cannot; dare, live by your strength and insight. But leave all for Him and take heart.

It is not your duty to worry about your future. But it is your duty to surrender your life to Him, and then do what you can and comfort yourself. It is shall be abundantly well. To you there is no hope, but to Him (God) all things are possible.

It is not yet late but it is a beginning of your life before God. He is going to start everything fresh in your life and those who are laughing at you, will be shock and ashamed.

Live as He wish but not your desire. It is not yet late at all. Only have hope in Him or trust Him. God is deeply willing to do everything for you. He is ever ready to welcome and comforted.

Do not think that your problem is not His problem or He does not mind. He is just watching that, He will reward those who seek Him. Consider and only say; let my life be dear to you, oh precious savior. Keep near to me and hold my hands.

I cannot; dare, live my life, my life is yours. Control everything about me and let me hope you care. My life is yours. I heard your voice calling me to come and have rest.

I have come; give me rest as your voice is saying. I cannot; dare, do for myself, Please give me rest. You are my hope; my shield and my redeemer. It is for you to act; my heart is breaking, my hope is in you, oh precious savior, I come to you.

If the world turns around and hope lost; my life is yours, Please Lord, do not leave, I cannot; dare, move without you. My life is yours. It is good that you press me.

Now I have seen what I can do for you. It is not my wish but by your wish, help me do according to your instruction and then do it right. My life is yours. I know you have learnt a lot and pray as well. What is your aim now and what do you want to do for Him? Is your life is His?

5. Hold me; I am weak

In fact, I cannot do for myself and I do not know how to do it. It is not my fault; I do not know how I must do it. I cannot; I cannot do for myself. I am weak and you are strong, please do it for me.

How will I live my life, if you leave me alone? It is difficult for me to move around; when I see your absences. Sometimes I feel your absence and thought you have left me alone.

I will make a mistake, if you leave me a moment. It is tough for me to go, when I feel your absence. Why have you forsake me; Lord? My enemies are all over, wanting to find fault on me.

I do not understand my weakness. I always wrong, when I want to do right. I cannot do for myself; unless you do for me. How can I dare, do for myself? Hold me please; I am weak.

When I am listening; I wrong, when I am writing I make mistake, when I am walking, I flop and find fault when I am looking. Who will rescue me from this weakness? It is only you; Lord. Hold me; I am weak. I cannot; dare, walk alone, please, do not leave me. It is not my fault, I do not understand; please hold me, I am weak. I cannot push; I do not know how to control myself. Please, hold me, I am weak.

I am fast to do wrong than good and wish flesh than the spirit. That is, my nature; I do not know why it is so with me? I consider nothing, unless I wrong in doing.

Please, hold me, I am weak. Your condition is not problem to God. Though, you are the worse sinner on the earth. His word to is come and let us reason together.

It is not late and your sin is ordinary before His grace. He can forgive the sin above sin, only if you will accept you're wrong and confess before Him. He is faithful to give all your sins and then cleanse you from it.

It does not matter your weakness or your sins that you been committed. God is able to forgive you by accepting and confess it to Him. He will not leave you to struggle alone and will not hide His face from you. Only recognize Him as your Lord and savior. He cares and mind than His apples of His eyes. You are dear to Him and will not forsake you. Be not afraid to come to

Him. He is merciful to forgive your sins and then cleanse you from all unrighteousness. You cannot live by your strength.

You will fail and be as nothing. Do not allow perplexities overcome you. You I cannot; dare, control the forces around the globe. Only allow His to rule and guide.

Your life cannot be accepted by God. If you dare, live by your own strength. It is not you but it is Him who works in us to His good pressure and what pleases Him. For by grace we have been saving, not by works, and then anyone should boast. You always need Christ to lead you. He is presence each minute to help and rescue sinners.

He is calling you with His tender voice; He is calling, He is calling, oh sinner come home. The beauty of His calling is that, He does not demand anything from you.

Your duty is to accept His voice and then go as He is calling you. Though, you are weak, but His grace is abundant for your weakness. Hold me; please, I am weak. Only accept it this way, He will accept you and then forgive you.

6. It is now dark in my life

What I am now seeing? So, this is how life is? It is now dark in my life. Sometimes life becomes worse and beyond compare. You always fail when you try.

You have attempted twice but you fail. It is now the third one but you cannot see it well. You ask yourself why? You do not understand the reason why you always fail, when you want to do something.

It cannot go well with you. You ask yourself why and why? Why me? You always fail, when you want to do. You start and it fall, no I cannot understand, no I cannot understand.

I will look into it, no, I will look into it. What can you do? Do you know the reason? Do you know what is going to happen, when you dare? It is dark in your life; yes, it is dark but do you know why?

There is nothing that will happen that has no reason. It is a reason and it is for the purpose. Who knows the end of each one's life? Who can tell the reason of such incidences that comes to life of each individual? Who knows the answer and who can tell reason? Darkness in life has reason and the purpose it serves. In this world, there is a night with a day.

The night serves as resting time for all human beings and it fit us for the day activities which are before us. So, it is in life, darkness time fit us for day time activities and keeps us fit continuously.

When your life turns around and things are not going well, do not be afraid, it is for your aid fitting you for future duty. This should not be a new thing but it is giving you a lesson for future progress and wellbeing. It is dark in your life; you cannot, dare, solve by your own strength.

It is for a reason and letting you on something necessary for your improvement. Do not, dare, make a mistake in trying times; Else, you will lost the purpose by which you been called to do.

If you dare, you will fail the Master. You cannot; dare, do something about it. Leave to God and be at peace. Darkness hours are experience time that will build you for good work and great glory in the near future of your life. It is not yet over but it is a lesson time. Do not think that it is gone and nothing can be done about it. Life is not easy as some people take it to be. It is more than a war between two forces of power.

It is needs giants to face and wise to control. But you cannot dare, make it without God. It is not over but there is hope. You need to consider your doings and manage it to the due time. It has an end, it will not last.

Do not fear and be discouraged. Do not say it is me again but give thanks to God and be at peace. You cannot do something about it but wait for God and have hope in Him.

It is not yet over. Let your prayer be oh Lord Fight for me, I cannot; dare, fight. This fight is for you but not me. Please, fight for yourself and do not include me.

It is your fight but not mine. Everyone have duty and purpose to achieve in this earth. Sin has caused a lot to count with; many things have change and our life have question and to be solve. Though, it is now dark in your life but it is not permanent; it will cease, Hope in God, it shall be well.

7. Show me the way

Lord I come to you just I am; I need your mercy and grace. Do not turn your eyes from me. I am yours, I cannot; dare, be alone. I am in dark in this state of my life.

I have go far end in my life. I am over age; I am getting old and my way is now end to do. I do not know what to do and where to go. Oh Lord, show me the way I should go.

I do not know where I should go and I not know the way forward. I see dark before me, I cannot go forward and I cannot come back. So, this is how it is in life? I do not know that life is beyond estimation.

Jesus savior pilots me on these waves of life. You are the pilot on the sea which rows and waves here and there. I cannot; dare, go alone without your presence. It is even tough to me to move on these waves of life.

How can I dare, go without you? Jesus savior shows me the way. The life is hard for me and I have spent my time without improvement. To me, there is no way out, you are the pilot of life, Jesus savior pilots me. I have come to the place where the waves are so strong to pass through, and I cannot go forward again, oh Lord Jesus, please hold my hands and lead me.

To me it is end, but to you it is now beginning; Precious savior pilots me. Loving shepherd protect your sheep, your power is stronger than every power. Please protect me from those enemies who are seeking my life.

The life is tough for me to live. I look to you, though my life is almost end and my hope is gone but you are strong and mighty to do. Please make it your own and rescue me from these troubles.

Show me the way; I am lost and have mixed my target. Nothing is late for you, please favor me and then settle my case. Jesus guide my way and lead me to home. That is, I need your comfort and grace in my life. The way is dark for me to move on; I cannot step forward, please I look to you and waiting. I cannot; dare, go without you, my hope is gone. Please, lead me home. It is fact that all your hope is gone. There is nothing left; to you the life has ended. It is true that you are suffering and all hopes are gone. Do not be afraid, it is not waste yet. If you have life; you have hope, it is not late yet. Your time is coming and you shall forget all your troubles and sufferings.

Only trust Him; He who create you. He will show you the way that you should go. Whether it is left or right, when you pass on it, it shall be well with you. It is yet waste but it is now beginning.

Thirst and see that, God is good, for those who run to Him are saved. It is not yet late at all. Have hope and live according to His wish, and all will be added to you. Oh shepherd of tender youth lead me on my way.

Let this be your prayer every day and keep on and keeping on. The mountains that you see always before you shall vanish and you will be set free and have your peace. God is ever ready to help and rescue us from our troubles. He loves the world and wishes the world life and progress. Woman can forget her child who she has given birth to, but God will not forget us even in the moment. He cares and shall show you the way you should go. Keep these messages and think about it day and night.

8. Do not leave me, Please!

It is still dark, nothing has change; I am now afraid. It seems I am about to die. Do not leave me, please! I cannot; dare, sleep alone. It is now day, everyone is going to his or her job. But my job has broken and do not know where to turn.

Do not leave me, please, I cannot; dare, be at home alone. It is far beyond my understanding, this life is hard for me, and I cannot hold it. Do not leave me, please, be my help.

I have struggle a lot but it is not okay for me. I am tire and I cannot continue again. Do not leave me, please, I cannot; dare, continue without you. It has overcome me and I am dying. Please, do not leave me, I cannot; dare, keep on.

I need you Lord and I cannot be alone without you. Come near to me and comfort me. Abide with me; night is fast falling, now I see darkness all over, I am afraid Lord abide with me. I need you every minute, please, do not leave me.

Be my friend and sit beside me, my heart is paining me. I cannot sit or sleep without you. Do not leave me, please! I cannot; dare, be alone. You are the friend in deed; your love is beauty. You have answered me. Now my heart is cheer. You have comfort me and have given me hope. Your name be the glory.

You always near when I call and always comfort when I am afraid. Oh Lord your love is kind and beautiful. My hope is in you, you are my shelter and protector. You love beauty and wish your children's well.

You know the thought that you are thinking towards us. It is not of evil but of peace and great hope. You love the world and gave your only son for our salvation.

We are grateful for that precious act. It is enough and nothing can be compared with. It is deeper than love itself and difficult to understand. You love man than yourself; it is very wonderful and great.

Who can understand your doing and know your ways. It is higher than the highest and bigger than the biggest. God love us no matter our condition as human beings.

He can forgive every sin that we have committed and then cleanse us from all unrighteousness. Your life is in His hands and He always remembered us as His, do not be afraid or discourage. I will be with you to the end of age. I will not leave you alone; you are mine until your old age, I will carry you on my shoulders.

He knows you from the womb of your mother and has set you to be his prophet for the nations. To pull down and rebuilt, you are His apples of His eyes, love and protected. It is not

His will to suffer you for want but it is for your aid and future greatness.

He does not want you to perish but come to repentance. He will not leave you or forsake you, you are dear to Him. He valued your life and wishes your life than death.

He always considers your suffering and takes note of it. He mind and always welcome you. Let's read Isaiah 43:1-7; read;

But now, thus says the LORD, who created you, O Jacob, And He who formed you, O Israel: "Fear not, for I have redeemed you; I have called you by your name; You are Mine.

2When you pass through the waters, I will be with you; And through the rivers, they shall not overflow you. When you walk through the fire, you shall not be burned, nor shall the flame scorch you.

3For I am the LORD your God, The Holy One of Israel, your Savior; I gave Egypt for your ransom, Ethiopia and Seba in your place.

4Since you were precious in my sight, you have been honored, And I have loved you; therefore I will give men for you, and people for your life.

5Fear not, for I am with you; I will bring your descendants from the east, and gather you from the west;

6I will say to the north, "give them up!' And to the south, "do not keep them back!' Bring my sons from afar, and My daughters from the ends of the earth—

7Everyone who is called by my name, whom I have created for my glory; I have formed him, yes, I have made him."

God is aware of our situations and there is nothing that comes without His permission. He will not leave us to suffer for our own but He will rescue and build us for new beginnings. Let your prayer be; Oh Lord; do not leave me and I cannot; dare, walk alone. Take my wish and live my life for me. It is yours, make it just as you want and be my guide always. I cannot; dare, live my life; please live it for me, for my life is yours.

Show me the way I should go, I cannot; dare, walk alone. Never think it is all gone or be discouraged because of waves you see. It shall stop and your peace will be still.

It is late, but you cannot; dare, walk alone. Let God lead, it shall be completely well. It is your time; be comfort and keep watch!

9. Move with Care

Life is not a race and it is not like the sea that is always busy. But it needs patience and control.

The mountain has trees but how can we find out the depth of the soil on top. So is life, we cannot find out the result.

But we can determine the outcome through the act of today's movement. Why are you rushing? Why are you compare or thinking you are late? A tree is not climbed by running; so as to life.

You cannot rush or run to make things done at a moment. As a song is arranged before singing, so life needs arrangement before it can be managed well. Do not think you are late and you need to do things fast to get a better life.

Days and years are set before us by God and life must track the same. You cannot do anything about it.

As the world consists of darkness and light, so as life be. And you cannot wake up one day and have all your needs on the same day.

As the world wasn't created in one day; so as life needs to be built with that series. The life needs to go by order and it must be built through days and years.

Be patient in whatever you are doing and take heart. Do not rush in speaking. Do not rush in eating; do not rush to answer a question and so on.

In fact, you cannot wash your hands with only soap without water. And again, you cannot go with a single leg and you cannot run with a single led.

It is impossible. You need to understand the series in life and how to cope with all situations.

What do I mean? Everyone needs wholesome characters for his or her life to earn profitable ends.

If you rush, you will miss the needed amenities and cause an accident to your life. Means you will either die before your time or lost a meaningful life.

Do not jump or run in life and again do not mark the time. But consider the way and the manner you behave.

You need to move like a clock move, but don't go before or after the clock. Means keep your time and make use of it.

As you cannot run on the muddy ground, so you cannot run in life. It is better to be late in life than to rush and fail in life.

As it is not lawful to use your two hands to eat; therefore, it is not lawful to rush or run in life.

Do not be too aggressive about your life to make things well. That is, do not force yourself to become rich.

But take time, and reason about the best way you can manage to the best of your wish. Why die before your time?

Do not rush, for you don't know what tomorrow holds for you. Be patient and keep on managing, then fulfill your goal and earn a good destiny.

10. Open your Eyes

You need to mind your business and value every little thing. Do not take things for granted.

Be serious in life and determine a positive result. Pick the little that have less attention and prepare it with days. Open your eyes and search for the best.

Do not mind to dig deep but consider every stage. Set the target but do not put aside the necessary tools for the life through rushing. Set your goal right but manage the rest.

Do not combine sugar and honey at the same time, but use them one after the other. Prepare yourself at each time and welcome negative and positive. Know the difference between day and night.

Do not misuse the time but make a profit each second. Control yourself at every hour and manage. Do things right but consider the outcome.

Do not move without considering your steps or do not move without your eyes.

Means take care and move. Arrange your kitchen and prepare your food. That is, be decent in all stages of life.

Do not use two knives at the same time. That is, do things one after the other. Do not combine dogs and cats in the same Apartment. That is, you cannot rear two different animals in one cage.

Do not play two songs at the same time. Means do not put yourself into trouble without preparation. Plan and do things in order.

Set the target but manage the target. That is, work towards your goal but do not put aside what benefit others and you.

Do not cut the guideline. Means do not overlook the laws and regulations. Do not talk when you are walking alone. That is, don't behave like a mad man. Cover your mouth when coughing. Means close your mouth when you are eating.

Do not combine salt and sugar at the same time. That is, do not combine lies with the truth.

Do not leave a stranger alone in your room. That is, do not trust the person you did not know well. Do not answer a word without understanding.

Do not combine oil and water as one substance. Do not use oil to wash your hand like water.

That is, do not replace bad for good or do not do things contrary to the law and order. Do not sit on somebody's chair without his or her consent. Means do not steal someone's property without his or her approval.

Do not mix two different oils for profit. Means do not cheat others for prosperities sake.

Do not forsake your old house in which you grow. Means do not disrespect your Mother or Father at their old age.

Do not compare two different ropes as the same. Means do not compare two different powers as the same. Go forward do not look back. That is, don't give up or be discouraged.

You need to dress up but do not forget your shoe. That is, don't overdress but dress decently.

Do not let your shoes make a noise when walking on the street. Means dress with no attention towards you or dress modestly with no comments.

Do not talk over time or more than the required hour. Means talk like a reasonable man but not as a fool.

Do not cross a small river on foot when it is raining. Means do not consider a small thing as of no value when you haven't experienced before.

Do not value yourself than others because of your beauty or exalt yourself concerning what you have, for you do not know the difference between today and tomorrow. Means you do not know what will happen today or tomorrow, so don't laugh at your friend.

Consider the poor and regard the aged at your harvest time. Means give to others who need your help today, for you don't know what tomorrow holds.

It is unnecessary to run in your bedroom or the living room. That is, it is not a good or wise thing to rush when you are eating.

Consider the wind and create windows at your room to keep it from heat. Means welcome people whom you did not know and they will bless you.

Respect the platform on which you are standing and do not run on it but consider its height, and then it will keep you from falling. Means respect those under you but do not disregard them; for they will let you prosper, and without them: you cannot stand.

Do not go before your master, but follow your master and learn from him. Always ask, if you don't know and don't be too known to cause your life into ruin.

Always try to do the best thing but do not exalt yourself about the good work done. Try to do the best of your time, when you are on duty at your workplace.

Do away laziness and be forceful. Consider every little thing, do not take it as light, else you will lose your dignity. Plan and do things in order. Never start your work without prayer. Be practical and manage any condition.

Do not be too high or do not be too simple, but be modest in the manner of no comments.

Manage to welcome everyone and speak well or be attentive to anyone who you communicate with.

Be ready always and set your goals well, do not discourage by circumstance but go forward.

Do not conclude your word without your viewers understanding, but make it clear to promote their peace.

Do not leave without concluding of your case, but settle it as it stands on you for peace. Know how to walk and talk in the house of God. Let your prayers be simple and reasonable.

Do not pray to please men, but pray from the heart and in humility. Stop conversation at the courtroom and consider your speech before the judge.

Respect and shut your mouth in the presence of the king. Do not be haste to answer a question but be considerate when answering. Do not push yourself into trouble when there is no trouble. Means keep yourself at all times from the words of others. Do not go before the thief or robber, else you will be adding by his or her punishment. Consider every act you proceed, and then have the good results. Do not say yes when the word is not true.

Do not shout when you are speaking to anybody. But consider your speech carefully in front of the rulers. Do not cry at the wedding premises even when you do not agree. But control yourself till the end. That is, be wise and do the right thing in the presence of the mass congregation.

Do not joke before a lion, whiles you don't have a leg to run. That is, do not annoy the king in his palace with a false act without redeemer or the advocate.

Do not put your leg on somebody's shoulder and laugh at the same time. Means do not cheat your brother and convince him with your false words of comfort. Do not mix salt and sugar in your mouth. That is, makes your words or speech clear for everyone to hear you well. Or do not deceive others by your words.

11. Make it on its Way

Do not close your eyes and walk, but open your eyes and see. Do the right thing.

Do the right thing, do not say yes, whiles the answer is no. do not run before your parents but run after them.

Do the right thing. Many people want to fill up their rooms and leave the whole building. Means do not hoard up by selfishness but give to others as you can.

Do the right thing. Respect men and wish them well. Do the right thing. Dress well, when leaving from home.

Arrange your bed before leaving. That is, do not close your eyes from your responsibilities. Do the right thing. Do not sweep your room and leave your corridor unprepared. That is, complete your responsibilities each day.

Do not put the light under the table, but on the table. Means do not cover what benefit others but share with them.

Do the right thing whiles you have life. Help the needy and rescue the perishing. Share the big and small at the hours of want. Go with charity and truth always, and then seek to help the weak.

Do the right thing! Do not look down on others because of your wealth. Do not eat to the bottom but leave the rest to the birds. That is, do not be selfish concerning what you have, but give to others who need your help.

Do not leave the old woman or man alone to struggle. Means do not close your eyes from the destitute or the weaker that need your donation. Do the right thing!

Do not take away the sightless stick to cause him or her fall. That is, do not cheat the stranger at your home about his or her needs.

Do the right thing! Do not pass through the window, whiles there is a door. Means do things according to the required measures. Do not sleep on the bed contrary to yours. Means do not take somebody's wife like yours.

Do not go and shout at the front of kings' palace out of consideration. That is, do not go beyond the demarcation or break the moral law.

Always seek to prevent war in the presence of your enemy and love at all times. Do the right thing! Keep on your donations and do not consider your giving by means of seeking the reward.

Help the stranger but consider your room, that is, serve the stranger as well but be vigilant.

Do not leave your keys for the one you do not know. Keep your eye on the ground and consider every weed.

That is, know how to deal with others for good but with the eyes open. Rejoice with those who are in good condition and at the same time mourn with those who are mourning.

Do not leave the food uncovered and do not give to the stranger the unwholesome food. Do not mislead the stranger by cheating. But honour the stranger with a good welcome.

Do not go before the stranger or after the stranger who did not know where to step his or her feet. Do the right thing! Set the time well to prevent lateness.

Do not delay the worker's payment to keep on their worries. But pay prompt their wages and to prevent curse.

Do not argue with your worker on his payment. Do not force your worker to work overtime but consider his strength and health.

Do not put your worker into trouble because of your wealth. Give a reasonable amount of payment to your worker to prevent murmuring against you.

Do not let your worker cry before to receiving his or her payment. Give and continue in giving, support and makes people laugh with a good heart.

Do not close your door and shout people's out from your presence. Means welcome people with a good heart and with love. Complete your work with the correct report and the best result.

Do not use your tools for making unnecessary things. But let your tools work excellently.

12. Why greediness today?

Oh what a world we live! Men have corrupted their ways. Many people love money than life and then cherish pleasure than God. We all have gone astray and each one for himself but not the other.

Everyone is looking for his or her own benefit than other and others seeking to be leader than servants. Many others love to cheat than to help. Greediness is all over the globe and the lies is the ruler of the day.

There is no consideration of each person and lies are been promote by bribing. Oh what a world we live? People love money than work and love bribe than wisdom.

There are a lot of challenges among us and then envying the fortunate who have been work faithfully for their produces. Oh what is going on the world today? Who is faithful?

Who is ready to stand for the truth? Who will live sufficient life and then accept his or her condition each day? It is times for us to fight for truth but not money; to stand for modest but not abundance of things. When the man gains the whole world and then loses his life, what is profit he will gain? What are you searching for? Why are you so greedy? Let consider our situation today as human beings.

Many of us as pupil cheat and mislead others who are weak because of selfish life we intend. Our away of life has become deception in all our doings. We cheat and pretend as good people and mock others by our lies.

What have you considered in your life? What do you do to the others around you? Are you greedy or selfish? This is the end time and everyone must watch out for his or her salvation.

We need to keep in mind what is before us. Everyone is going to face his or her reward due to the work done. We are all hurry to get wealth as quick as possible. But what will be the end?

Let consider our doings and then change from wrong acts. What are we doing to ourselves today? Cheating and murdering one and another.

Greediness cannot bear good fruit but leads to death. We must accept whatever we have and then give thanks to God. Do not love the world; neither things of the world, the world and the things are passing away; yet the one who love God shall live. You must accept your condition and things you have is all seasons. Do not be hurry to get wealth but wait upon the Lord and then be strong.

Put away envy and do your honest work; it shall be well. Do not force yourself to be rich; yet gather it little by little to keep your-self from damage. It is better to be poor and live peaceful life than to be rich and then ruin your life.

Do not hoard up through greediness but accept your little belongings and then stay safe and peaceful. Greediness comes by envy and it makes fruit through selfishness.

Do not follow wealth but wisdom to fulfill your mission with honest and then harvest abundant life. Let us keep in mind that everyone will receive the reward of the deeds exhibited. Do not compare yourself with others, neither considers their wealth. Yet keep yourself and accept your belongings.

Now it is time to keep yourself well and then do away greediness and then save your soul from eternal doom. Do not look to others concerning their wealth, but look to God and be saved.

13. The peak time

The time is far spent and days are now left a few. We have reached the top of the mountain and there is no way to descend or come down. The world has reached the peak point and the things are now falling apart.

There is no future again for those who hope in today's world, but future for those who hope for the coming one. When will you come out from your wrong doings? Why are you wasting your time on the fake things?

There is no time for jokes and no time for envying. We are in the horrible state in the world history today. The air that is blowing, show the end of today's world.

Many people are seeking for high positions and abundant wealth. There is no care in the way that people live; that is many people live as they wish and think is their rights. Others cheat and think it is okay.

There are wars and rumor of wars. Challenges are all over on the globe and false reports are rampant. There are noise successes everywhere which many people think is a blessing to own houses and luxury cars to proof your acceptance of God. This has no basic proof concerning blesses of God. So many people are seeking wealth instead God and their future position.

Oh! Will you mind to change your thoughts and your ways that seems good in your sight? There are a lot of wickedness's going on. Many people do not mind to get wealth through killings of weak ones.

Robberies are all over the globe; stealing and killing at the same time. Many people are seeking wealth unlawful ways and also killing innocent people.

There are corruptions everywhere; false teachers and prophets allover. People are confused to live and others are broken by false messages. Many others want to live a cheap life and make money without law.

The world leaders are hoarding up belongings for their families and their own interest. Selfishness has gain position than selfless. Many people are drinking wine and make merry without consideration of honest life. Oh world! When will you consider God and your life? Why loving world than your life? When shall you repent from your wrong doings? Have you consider the coming age? Where will you stand at the end? Do not climb the tree with your back. Means do not live by the way that seems good in your own sight.

Yet, live according to the setout regulations and then prevent damage at the end. The world is running out; there are noises everywhere, people are fighting for positions.

Now many people want to live anyhow and eat anyhow and drink anyhow. Some of us want to dress anyhow and then live without consideration.

Money has bought many peoples mind and some of them are control by wine. Darkness's are across everywhere and people love bribe than honest work. Many people pretend and deceive by their acts.

Some of us pretend as Christians but follow the devil directions. False doctrines are growing each day and night. People love lies than truth and then cherish jokes than awareness.

There are many fake pastors and prophets today making money through greediness; pretending like Christ followers but denial of the true worship and godliness. But they have many followers; praising them through their lies. Some Women are their supporters praising them by senseless acts and lacks of knowledge of God.

Many people have taken worship of God light and then doing what they think is right at their own estimation. There are many jokers in the world today; thinking that they are worshipping God in truth.

So many pastors mislead people by their false message. Others too deceive to gain money. There are a lot of wickedness's going on in the world today. Oh! What are you looking for?

Why are you wasting your time on the goods of the world? Here is not our home; the world is going to the end.

We all need to behave well and then keep ourselves from corruption in this world. We are in the probation time and the time of grace. Let us watch out and keep watch for we do not know the time of visitation.

14. No time again

Will this world live any longer again? Will it remain the same as this? Is there any time again for pleasure and goodness? What will be the end situation of this world?

The time is far spent and there is no time again. Who knows the end situation of this world? Who can tell the result of this world history? What will be the condition?

I mean how will this end will be look like? There is no time again; no time for jokes, no time for singing and dancing. No time for enjoyment and no time for discussing issues.

Oh my dear! Is this your concern? Have you thought of it? Do you mind to live a worthy life? What do you think? What is your work? Who do you believe?

There is no time again. The days are now gone and the years is finish. We are on the verge of this world history. Oh dear! Will you mind?

Many people think that, there is no judgment and others also always say this life is all; there is no other time again ahead of us. Some even think that, there is no accountability anywhere after this life. Some also think that, there is a place by which we can live there or migrate to for peaceful atmosphere.

There are many thoughts going on in people's lives. Is there any hope after this life or is there any place to go after this era? If there is no other life after this life, then how wicked will be punish or receive their reward?

Where will the righteous live or receive their reward? It is time for this world to go and for the new world to come which dwells righteousness and peace. What have you consider or noticed?

The history of this world is now almost over and the things are turning round without notice. Many people think that, it shall be the same as it was at the beginning.

What I mine going to receive after this life? When will this world go over? How will it be? Who can stand? What will be the end?

Everyone will receive his or her reward according to the work done. It is now time for each and every one must watch out. There is no time again for frivolous talks and unnecessary argument. We must cease from bragging and work on our own salvation. The time is almost finished; we are in probation and all signals are calling us to come out from Babylon.

Why many people are seeking for world goods instead of eternal life? We have lost the idea by which we were created for as human beings. We all follow weeds instead of gold and seeking for food instead of life.

We must watch out and then prepare ourselves for the coming of the Master. There is no time again. We need to turn from our wrong doings and then seek for what is right and truth for our souls. What will be the end of this journey? What I mine going to receive at the end? There are noise everywhere; people roaming about seeking for money and material things.

Many people have forgotten themselves and the purpose they were created for, because of money. Many people seeking money beyond the barrier. Means they were seeking money regardless law and the right way. There is no time again; let seek the Lord at this moment of the world.

15. Where are you going?

Oh! Is this how you want your life at this moment of the world history? Where are you heading towards? Why have you taken the world into your bosom? What have you dress? How do you want your life?

Is smoking well for your health? Then why are you smoking? Is strong wine helpful? Then why are you drinking strong wine? Will this help your life at the end?

Where are you heading towards? What will these things do for you? What will women do for you? Why are you chasing men? Is this how you want your life? When will you stop these things?

Will this benefit you? What are you doing to yourself? When will you consider all these things that you are doing? Have you considered the outcome?

What do you think it will be? When will you stop those acts? Where are you going? My dear brother, this not good time and this is not the time for jokes. What will these things do for you? Why die before your time? You still follow your wish instead of the law requirements. Why this life and wish? Please turn from going that direction. Set a right step for your foot and then position yourself well.

For where you are going is wrong direction. Have you asked someone concerning where you are going? What answer did that person gave to you? He has already been there before.

Oh dear! You need to know more about life and where you are going. Do not struggle for goods but struggle for correct life and how you will earn knowledge for life.

Do you know more about life? Have you asked for the way you should go? How have you done it? What make the results? You need to think and ask for what you do not know.

Build yourself well and do things right. Where are you going? Do not miss the way; the truth and the life because of money. Never abuse yourself for the sake of money and do not act as if you do not have mind.

You need to consider anything that you are doing. Then ask yourself about the results of whatever you are doing. Whatever the direction, you must know the outcome. Do not follow money but follow wisdom and eschew evil. Always know the place you are going and then what you are going to do.

Means know the outcome of whatever you are doing. This is not good time. We are on the verge of this world and all things are calling us to prepare and then meet the Master.

What life do you want to make and what have you considered? Will this be better for you? Do not follow many people and sin, yet know how to comport yourself among the multitude.

Know where to turn and know what to do at every hour. Do not waste time or misuse it for no improvement. It is not good time. You must keep yourself from deceptions.

Cease from that thing you think is good without considering the law. Change your direction and then prepare yourself to suit the time. Make right path for your foot and turn from where you are going. It is not good time. You think for yourself and keep yourself from wrong doing. Where are you going? Will it be a help?

16. It is a test time

Now is the time of grace and time of salvation. We are in the probation and there is no time again. We are in the test time and probation. The world is now dark and it is in sad condition than ever before.

There are violence's everywhere on this earth. Now, many people are wicked than ever before since entry of the sin. Many people do not care their life. Others keep on in killings their brothers.

Theft has increase and murder follow suit by those robbers. Wickedness has hoard up and lie displays in the air always. People do not fear God again and mind mercy.

Bribes are license for the increase of the wealth. There is no law working on the on today in people's lives. Many people love cheating than working for.

Many of the youth are now fornicating day and night. Bad dressings are all over causing harm to the mind of many people. Sin has increase than ever before and many people are bathing it like water. These acts are calling us to meet our Lord in air. It is a test time and trying moments for all human beings. For this reason many people will be discourage because of rampant murdering. Now knowledge has increased but many people lack understanding.

All these things are calling us to be ready for the Master return. It is a test time, who will pass this test and then win the crown. Many people's mind has polluted and darkens; by which there is no light at all.

Today's murdering are the signs of the end time. Many people do not understand the reasons why it is so. Do not be confuse about these matters, it must come to prove the true saying of Christ. The devil wants many people to be on his part and then deceive many as he can. The world has changed and it is going to destroy. There are dominant of wickedness of the globe today sounding everywhere.

Money is the king ruling on everyone's mind and then controlling people to do foolish things. Selfishness has grown to it height, but there is no proper improvement as which they want. Why? What is the end of these things? What is the benefit of it? All these things are testing of our faithfulness to God. It is a hard times and the testing of our faith in God. There are wars and rumor of wars pointing to the peak time of today's world situation.

What have you considered? How prepared are you? When shall you repent from your wickedness? Will you continuing in your wickedness? Thief comes to steal and kill; our situation in the world today is horrible.

What are we hearing and what are we seeing? Killings are all over and people are dying without hope. We are in the testing time.

There is no mercy in the world today. Many people are mad in mind because of money. But it is a testing time; we are all in balance, weighing us to see our fitness and honesty. Who shall stand? Who will be fitted at the end? It is a test time. The fear of Lord is out from men and there is no fear of God again. Everyone is going to receive his or her reward at the end according to the work done. It is a test time, and there is no time again. What will be your portion? Will you mind?

17. What are you doing?

What are you waiting for and what are you doing? Have you considered your doings? Do you mind your actions today? Are you on the track? Do you follow your mind or God?

What are your actions? Are you faithful? If you look around, what do you see? What is your action towards that? Oh! What are we seeing today and what is going on?

Will you continue in this? When will you repent? Why are you still misleading people? Why are you still lying? When will you stop deceiving? Will you continue in fornication? When will you stop stealing?

Many people do not know when they will be paid through their work. What salary are they going to receive? Will it be fair or not? But it depends on the work they did. You will be paid according to your doings or work.

So, why don't you do the right work or thing? Is what you are doing fair or truthful? What have you considered or noticed? What do you think? Is it true that you did it according to the requirements? Oh dear. You must know more than you know and consider your direction. What is your aim? Where are you focusing? Will it be better for you? What have considered and know? Will this be better when you try?

Is that dress good to wear? Will that food help your health? What is your mind? What do you imagine? What will be the end? Do not pretend as you know everything, but let others teach you. Be a learner and teacher as well.

Do not raise your head up or despise others opinion. Come down and do your best as it suit the occasion. Learn to share and keep on sharing with others.

Do something for recognition with good report. Stop cheating in work with others and then do your honest part. It is not good era, yet it is a trying time with dangerous hours. Is what you are doing good or bad?

What have you noticed? Many people have turned their back to God and doing what they wish. Others prefer lies to truth and wish to cheat than support. They love bribe than sacrifice and then deceive than beauty. They love by mouth but fails in action. Others love money than life and love wealth than truth. When will you continue in these things? Oh keeper! What is the time now? Why are you joking in these bad times? What are you doing? Is it right or wrong? Will it help you?

Many women have taken this world into their bosom and doing a lot of horrible things. They have regardless their life and respect. They have putting their eyes on their back and moving forward without eyes.

Means they are intentionally doing wrong as without law in life. What are you doing? Will this be good results? My sister, do you know what you are doing?

Do you know the end? Will you be accepted by the Master? When will you repent from those actions? Do not take the world or things of the world into your bosom. Yet manage the life according to the regulations or laid down rules, and then prevent your life from ruin.

What are you doing? Means are you on the right path or living as you suppose to live? If not, change from those wrong doings and then save your life from eternal doom. It is not good time; will you consider and then stop harming yourself at the end?

18. When will you return?

Will you continuing doing evil? Where will this end you? When will you return or stop doing wrong? Ask yourself who is controlling me? Is what I am doing right?

What will be the result? Where I mine going to stand? What will be my reward? Many people keep on doing evil and others are murdering with their mouth.

There are shadows across the sky and darkness is taking over the world. Many people are crying and some are dying without hope. What is coming to this world?

Is there any hope? What will happen in the next hour? Who can tell the outcome? It seems you still regardless the time and you do not mind what are coming.

Shall you continue in these things? Be patient in life and never rush at this moment. But prepare yourself always and seek the truth. When will you return?

Do you want to follow wisdom or foolishness? What have you decide? Where are you making your direction? Will that journey help you? Why don't find out the end of this journey you have decided? You have gone far please; return it is not too late.

It shall be well and there is hope, only if you will return from your wrongs. It is not late at all; He (Christ) is waiting for you and wishes you well. Do not look at the waves, you just return to Him.

He knows the thoughts and the plan He have prepared for you. It is of hope and great expectation. Change your style of living and build yourself well.

Return, oh! Backslider son; your Father is calling you. He is afraid for you and love to save and comfort you. When will you return? Do not wait for long, He is calling and waiting for you.

Though, many people are seeking for wealth and belongings. Others are killing for properties, but what will be the results? It is not late, come oh backsliding son. Return and come home son; you are dear to Me, I die for you and have considered and chosen you! When will you return my dear? You have been favored and loved. You are dear to Me. I have loved you with an everlasting love, said the Lord. You are always present in my eyes.

Do not fear and be not dismay, I am always with you till the end of time. You are dear to me and wish you well. This is the word of God to us.

We have made this world sad and uncomfortable. We are all doing what we like and regardless the laws of God. You do not fear to sin and does not mind to do wrong.

Now the world is filling with violence and darkness all over the globe. The time is far spent and days are no more. Oh! How long will this continue and how long will you repent? When will these last? Do you fear God? When will you return? We love money than wellbeing and wish selfishness than development and good character. It is time for you to return from wrong doings and change your steps. We are in the end time and anything can happen. We do not know what is before us, but we can prepare for any outcome. Make good steps for your feet and turn from those evil works and then fear God. When will you return?

19. He is coming

We are almost home; the King is coming to reward everyone according to his work. He is coming. Have you prepared for His return? Will you be accepted when He comes?

What will be your reward? You need ask yourself about these questions. The world is now in the balance, weighing to find out the weight of violence it had.

Whether it's must stay or not. What will be the results? We are on border of the world; waiting for rescue and comfort. The wind that is blowing is the sign of His coming.

Look, He is coming on the cloud and everyone will see Him. The world will be silent about Him and all the people will be amaze of Him. Why many wickedness today?

Why rampant robberies today? Why too much cheating all over the globe? Why greediness all over the world? Why killings and lies everywhere on the globe.

Why war and rumor of wars everywhere in the world? Why misunderstanding in all the group of people in the world? Why false prophets everywhere in the world? All these things are callings us to meet the King in the air. He is coming! The world has reached the highest height of the sin.

Darkness has covered all the face of the world. There is no light to see ahead, darkness is all over the world. Many people love money and others are greedy in seeking wealth.

What do you see and what are you saying about it? Will people continue in wickedness? When shall all these things last? What are you doing? Violence upon violence and killing upon killings are going on.

When shall all these things cease? These are the signs of His coming calling us to repent form our wrong doings. In fact, those things that are going on in the world today are calling us to prepare and meet our Lord in air.

These should not be surprise but it must be a lesson to us. This shows the condition of this world and what the sin of our first parents has brought to us. Everyone must prepare and to be ready for the bad day. For what we see and hear are calling us to be alert. Is your salvation dear to you? How serious are you in this time of crisis? What are you doing to save your life? Will you be able to come out? The world has reach in the deepest stage in sin.

It is time for God to do way sin and punish those who are involved. What brought flood in the Noah's time? Now the Spirit of God is ceasing from striving with men, because they are flesh.

Our days have shorting and there is sound again in our members. Our conditions as human beings are horrible and it needs disciple through the acts of God.

Now the wickedness in the world today is great. The fear of God has gone from men and there is no comfort in the world today. In fact, our condition in the world today is terrible.

People love to sin than to do well and now madness has fill up in the mind of men. Women has destroy the beauty this world. Many of them wish to do wrong than good.

They have made this world dark and gloomy because of their wearing and appearances. They have block good knowledge and understanding and have made world unfair. When will they repent from their short comings? Now men follow suit and wish them on wrong doings. Violence are all over the world and people love to sin than to do well.

Oh! When shall these things end? Who will consider his or her deeds and then stop wrong doings. Oh world! Christ Jesus is coming to pay each work done.

What have you notice? What are you doing? Will you continue in these wrong acts? In fact, these days are dangerous for men and all those who dwell on the earth today.

Our thoughts are evil continuously and our doings are evil every day. Who is ready for Christ return? Who have prepared to meet Him? Look, He is coming with the cloud and His Angels are with Him. Now, it is time for us to repent from our wrong doings and set straight path for our feet.

We are not in good times, anything can happen? What is your goal? Where are you focusing? Keeper, what is the time now? It is now probation. We are in the time of grace and there is no time again? What will be your reward? Oh keeper! Prepare and meet your Lord. Will you consider this message?

What are you doing about it? Is your life dear to you? When will you repent from your wrong doings? Remember, we are in the probation time, and there is no time again. Prepare to meet your God in air.

For Good Living; salvation and Knowledge Gain!
B. B. S. LIFE BOOKS.
Making the Life with the Life Giver Page

Also by Bernard Benson Sarfo

The Fact Among Facts (1st)
The Fact Among Facts

Standalone
The Youth Murderer
Be Original Not a Copy
The Christians Science or Scholarship
Precious than Paradise
Habit Makes Future
A shelter from storm and rain
The Science of Life
The Strongest Lion Knockback
The Perfect and Inspiring City
Above Hope, Faith and Love
The Hero's Brave Decisions
The Weakest Among Plants
The Hero's Brave Decisions
Doing Above The Ability
The Wisdom Beyond Power And Greatness

Heavier Than the Heavens
The Academics Brains and Recreation Logics
The Strange Voice
The Chaotic World
Don't Miss Your Flight
Let the Nations Ponder
You Are Your Thoughts
I AM has sent me to you
Life Tools
The Fact Among Facts
You Are Glorified
The Life Cinema
The Victims of Lifelong Slavery
The Beauty behind Her Ladyship
The Gorgeous and Vigorous City
What Is His Name?
Making the Life with the Life Giver

About the Author

Bernard Benson Sarfo is an acquainted architectural designer and a motivational speaker. He is a gifted teacher who continues to motivate and encourage many.

Read more at https://www.amazon.com//author/bbslifebooks.